# Forward

This cookbook contains 24 eggless, vegetari⟨ cupcakes and muffins. The recipes in this bo⟨ without eggs and are very easy for you to us⟨ regular or Greek yogurt are good egg replac⟨ ⟩ ... ⟨ddition to commercial egg replacers like Bob's Red Mill or Ener-g. There is of course some chemistry involved in baking eggless which requires the right kind and amounts of fats as well as the right amounts of flour. Cream cheese, bananas, chocolate and acids also improve the success of your eggless baking. When baking muffins, I also like to use ground flax seed meal, which adds great nutrition in addition to helping with egg replacement.

In addition to being eggless, these recipes are peanut-free and lacto vegetarian as they contain dairy, but do not contain eggs.

These recipes have been developed over the past 13 years and have been tested so that you too can bake eggless!

Baking Tip: Use paper liners for these cupcakes and muffins.

This book is the second in a series of cookbooks on eggless baking. The first being, **Cakes and Cheesecakes**.

# Table of Contents

1. Pumpkin Spice Cupcakes ----------------------------3

2. Coconut Cupcakes -------------------------------------5

3. Chocolate Cupcakes---------------------------------8

4. Chocolate Cannoli Cupcakes-------------------------11

5. Mocha Cupcakes -------------------------------------14

6. Key Lime Pie Cupcakes-------------------------------16

7. Red Velvet Cupcakes---------------------------------18

8. Vanilla Cupcakes-------------------------------------21

9. Vanilla White Chocolate Cupcakes------------------23

10. Strawberry Cupcakes -------------------------------26

11. Quick and Easy Cupcakes--------------------------28

12. Maple Oat Muffins-----------------------------------30

13. Coconut Lime Muffins-------------------------------32

14. Pumpkin Whole Wheat Muffins--------------------34

15. Raspberry Lemon Muffins --------------------------36

16. Lemon Blueberry Muffins ---------------------------38

17. Blueberry White Chocolate Muffins---------------40

18. Banana Chocolate Chip Muffins------------------42

19. Whole Wheat Banana Chip Muffins --------------44

20. Maple Banana Muffins ------------------------------46

21. Banana Oat Muffins --------------------------------48

22. Pumpkin Chocolate Chip Muffins -----------------50

23. Blueberry Oat Muffins-------------------------------52

24. Mango Blueberry Oat Muffins---------------------54

Inspiration ----------------------------------------------56

About the Author------------------------------------------57

# 1. Pumpkin Spice Cupcakes

When it is fall, it is Pumpkin everything!! This Pumpkin Spice Cupcake recipe will be a new addition to add to your fall favourites! I made the frosting a bit stiffer than my usual cream cheese frosting to help it hold better for decorating.

Ingredients:

| | | | |
|---|---|---|---|
| 1/4 cup softened butter | 2 cups flour | 1/4 tsp allspice | 3 cups icing sugar |
| 1 cup white sugar | 2 tsp baking powder | 3/4 cup milk | |
| 1/4 cup brown sugar | 1/2 tsp baking soda | 125g softened cream cheese | |
| 1/4 cup canola oil | 1/4 tsp salt | 1/4 cup softened butter | |
| 1 and 1/2 cups pumpkin puree | 1 tsp cinnamon | 1/2 tsp vanilla | |
| 1/2 cup plain yogurt | 1/4 tsp nutmeg | pinch salt | |

# Pumpkin Spice Cupcakes

Cream together butter and sugar:
   1/4 cup softened butter
   1 cup white sugar
   1/4 cup brown sugar

Then mix in:
   1/4 cup canola or vegetable oil

Then add and mix in:
   1 and 1/2 cups pumpkin puree
   1/2 cup plain unsweetened yogurt (equal to 2 eggs)

In a separate bowl, sift together dry ingredients:
   2 cups flour
   2 tsp baking powder
   1/2 tsp baking soda
   1/4 tsp salt
   1 tsp cinnamon
   1/4 tsp nutmeg
   1/4 tsp allspice

Alternate adding the dry ingredients into the batter with the milk and mix until incorporated:
   3/4 cup milk

Bake at 350 degrees F for approximately 20 minutes in paper-lined cupcake tins. Cool and then frost. Makes 18.

## Cream cheese Frosting
   1/2 pkg softened cream cheese (equal to 125g)
   1/4 cup softened butter
   1/2 tsp vanilla
   pinch of salt
   3 cups icing sugar (more if needed)

Beat the cream cheese, butter, salt and vanilla. Then add in approximately 3 cups icing sugar until the frosting is the consistency you want. Frost the cooled cupcakes.

4

# 2. Coconut Cupcakes

I had a bit of coconut milk leftover from another recipe and was inspired to make something coconut-y. I had coconut flakes in the fridge as well, so I decided to make coconut cupcakes. They are topped with cream cheese frosting but they would also be good with either a traditional butter cream or even whipped cream. Yum!

Ingredients:

| | | |
|---|---|---|
| 1/4 cup softened butter | 2 cups flour | 250g softened cream cheese |
| 1 and 1/4 cups sugar | 2 tsp baking powder | 1 tsp vanilla |
| 1/4 cup canola oil | 1/4 tsp salt | pinch salt |
| 1 tsp vanilla | 1/2 cup coconut milk | 3 cups icing sugar |
| 1/2 cup plain yogurt | 1/2 cup milk | 1 cup toasted coconut |
| 1/2 cup unsweetened coconut | 1/4 cup softened butter | |

## Coconut Cupcakes

Cream together:
 1/4 cup softened butter
 1 and 1/4 cups sugar

Then add and mix well:
 1/4 cup canola or vegetable oil
 1 tsp vanilla
 1/2 cup plain unsweetened yogurt (or prepared egg replacer equal to 2 eggs)
 1/2 cup unsweetened coconut

Sift dry ingredients in a separate bowl:
 2 cups flour
 2 tsp baking powder
 1/4 tsp salt

Alternate adding the dry ingredients with the milk into the batter:
 1/2 cup coconut milk
 1/2 cup milk

Mix well. Spoon into paper-lined cupcake tins and bake at 350 degrees F for approximately 20-22 minutes. Makes 12-14. Cool and then frost.

## Cream Cheese Frosting

Mix together, adding the icing sugar in last:
 1/4 cup softened butter
 1 pkg softened cream cheese (250g)
 1 tsp vanilla
 pinch salt
 3 cup icing sugar (or more if needed)

Frost the cooled cupcakes and top with: 1 cup toasted coconut.

# 3. Chocolate Cupcakes

These cupcakes are made from a recipe I adapted using a well known Wacky Cake recipe. These work without an egg replacer. They can be topped with many different frostings and will be a family, and especially kid, favourite.

Ingredients:

| 3 cups flour | 3/4 cup oil | 1/2 cup cocoa powder |
|---|---|---|
| 2 cups sugar | 2 tsp vanilla | 1 tsp vanilla |
| 3/4 cup cocoa powder | 2 tsp vinegar | pinch salt |
| 2 tsp baking powder | 1 cup water | 4 tbsp milk |
| 1 tsp baking soda | 1 cup milk | 3 cups icing sugar |
| 1 tsp salt | 3/4 cup softened butter | |

## Chocolate Cupcakes

Combine Dry Ingredients:
   3 cups flour
   2 cups sugar
   3/4 cup cocoa powder
   2 tsp baking powder
   1 tsp baking soda
   1 tsp salt

Mix and make a well. In the well add:
   3/4 cup vegetable or canola oil
   2 tsp vanilla
   2 tsp vinegar
   1 cup water
   1 cup milk

Mix really well with a mixer. This makes 20 good size cupcakes. Bake at 350 degrees F for approximately 20 minutes in paper-lined cupcake tins.

## Chocolate Frosting

3/4 cup softened butter
1/2 cup cocoa powder
1 tsp vanilla
pinch salt
4 tbsp milk
3 cups icing sugar (more if needed)

Cream the butter and then add in the cocoa, vanilla, salt, milk and icing sugar. Beat until fluffy and then frost the cooled cupcakes.

Note: If you want a lot of frosting, make an extra half batch of this recipe.

# 4. Chocolate Cannoli Cupcakes

These Chocolate Cannoli Cupcakes are inspired by an Italian dessert called Cannoli's. They take a bit of extra time to make the filling, but they are yummy! This uses my Chocolate Cupcake recipe and does not require an egg replacer.

Ingredients:

| | | |
|---|---|---|
| 3 cups flour | 2 tsp vanilla | 1 tsp vanilla |
| 2 cups sugar | 2 tsp vinegar | 2 cups heavy cream (35%) |
| 3/4 cup cocoa powder | 1 cup water | 1/4 cup icing sugar |
| 2 tsp baking powder | 1 cup milk | 2 tbsp prepared gelatine (optional) |
| 1 tsp baking soda | 1 cup Ricotta cheese | mini chocolate chips |
| 1 tsp salt | 1/4 cup white sugar | |
| 3/4 cup oil | 1 tbsp cocoa powder | |

First make **Chocolate Cupcake** recipe.

Combine Dry Ingredients:
  3 cups flour
  2 cups sugar
  3/4 cup cocoa powder
  2 tsp baking powder
  1 tsp baking soda
  1 tsp salt

Mix and make a well. In the well add:
  3/4 cup vegetable or canola oil
  2 tsp vanilla
  2 tsp vinegar
  1 cup water
  1 cup milk

Mix really well with a mixer. This makes 20 good size cupcakes. Bake at 350 degrees F for approximately 20 minutes in paper-lined cupcake tins.

## Chocolate Cannoli Filling

  1 cup Ricotta cheese
  1/4 cup white sugar
  1 tbsp cocoa powder
  1 tsp vanilla

Mix all ingredients together really well with a hand mixer. Fill a pastry bag with the cream.

Poke a hole in each of the cooled cupcakes about 3/4 of the way down. I use the end of a wooden spoon. Fill gently. The filling will pop out of the top when full.

Top with your favourite frosting or you can use whipped cream.

At this point, they will look like this:

## Whipped Cream

2 cups whipping cream (35%)
1/4 cup icing sugar

Beat the cream and gradually add the sugar while beating. Beat until it is just beyond soft peaks.

Note: I add 2 tbsp of prepared gelatine to stabilize my whipping cream while the cream is whipping.

Top with mini chocolate chips!

# 5. Mocha Cupcakes

This recipe has coffee added to my Chocolate Cupcake recipe to make Mocha Cupcakes. The coffee flavour definitely comes through without being overpowering. These do not require an egg replacer. This recipes makes 18-20 cupcakes.

Ingredients:

| 3 cups flour | 3/4 cup oil | 1 cup softened butter |
|---|---|---|
| 2 cups sugar | 2 tsp vanilla | 1 tsp vanilla |
| 3/4 cup cocoa powder | 2 tsp vinegar | 2 tbsp prepared coffee |
| 2 tsp baking powder | 1 cup milk | 3 cups icing sugar |
| 1 tsp baking soda | 1 cup prepared coffee | |
| 1 tsp salt | 4 tbsp cocoa powder | |

## Mocha Cupcakes

Sift together:
   3 cups flour
   2 cups sugar
   3/4 cup cocoa powder
   2 tsp baking powder
   1 tsp baking soda
   1 tsp salt

Make a well and add all of the wet ingredients:
   3/4 cup vegetable or canola oil
   2 tsp vanilla
   2 tsp vinegar
   1 cup milk
   1 cup prepared coffee

Using a mixer, blend well. Fill paper-lined cupcake tins two-thirds full. Bake at 350 degrees F for approximately 20 minutes.

## Mocha Frosting
   4 tbsp cocoa powder
   1 cup softened butter
   1 tsp vanilla
   2 tbsp prepared coffee
   3 cups icing sugar (more if needed)
Adding the icing sugar in last, blend the ingredients until light and fluffy using a mixer. Frost the cooled cupcakes.

15

# 6. Key Lime Pie Cupcakes

Girls night calls for a new cupcake recipe!! I saw a recipe for these on Pinterest and figured this recipe would work due to the acid of the lime as well as the buttermilk. This recipe originally called for all butter but I find the product will crumble easily when all butter is used so I replaced half of the butter with canola oil. I also bumped up the flour a little bit as well. These turned out really well with a great taste and texture!

Ingredients:

| | | | |
|---|---|---|---|
| 1/4 cup softened butter | 1 tbsp lime zest | 3/4 cup butter-milk | 1 tsp lime zest |
| 1 and 1/4 cups sugar | green food colouring (optional) | 1/4 cup milk | 1/2 tsp vanilla |
| 1/4 cup oil | 2 cups flour | 250g softened cream cheese | 3 cups icing sugar |
| 1/2 cup plain yogurt | 1 and 1/2 tsp baking powder | 1/2 cup softened butter | |
| 3 tbsp lime juice | 1/4 tsp salt | 1 tbsp lime juice | |

# Key Lime Pie Cupcakes

Cream together:
  1/4 cup softened butter
  1 and 1/4 cups sugar

Then add and mix well:
  1/4 cup canola or vegetable oil
  1/2 cup plain unsweetened yogurt (or egg replacer equal to 2 eggs)
  3 tbsp lime juice
  1 tbsp lime zest
  couple of drops green food colouring (optional)

In a separate bowl combine dry ingredients:
  2 cups flour
  1 and 1/2 tsp baking powder
  1/4 tsp salt

In a large measuring cup mix together:
  3/4 cup buttermilk
  1/4 cup milk

Alternate adding the dry ingredients and the milk mixture into the batter until mixed well. Scoop into paper-lined cupcake tins and bake at 350 degrees F for 20-25 minutes. Cool. Makes 12-14.

## Cream Cheese Lime Frosting
Cream together:
  1 pkg softened cream cheese (250g)
  1/2 cup softened butter

Then add:
  1 tbsp lime juice
  1 tsp lime zest
  1/2 tsp vanilla
  3 cups icing sugar (more if needed)
Beat until fluffy. Frost cooled cupcakes. Tip: If the frosting is a bit runny, you can refrigerate for an hour before icing the cupcakes.

# 7. Red Velvet Cupcakes

Red Velvet Cupcakes are generally adored by all but the thought of adding that much red food colouring (up to 2 tbsp!) makes me a little nervous. So, I went in search of a natural red food dye and did not come up with anything in my local city except beet root powder. The batter turned out a nice deep red colour but once baked the cupcakes turned a light brown due to the reaction of the beet root while baking. So unfortunately the beet root did not result in a colour worthy of the term "red velvet".

So, I decided to make them with red food colouring. (Adding 3 tbsp of cocoa powder helps darken the red without adding the usual amount of food dye.) This is a rare treat and not something I would make often.

Ingredients:

| 2 cups flour | 3 tbsp cocoa powder | 2 tsp vanilla | pinch salt |
|---|---|---|---|
| 1 and 1/2 cups sugar | 3/4 cup oil | red food colouring | 3 cups icing sugar |
| 1 tsp baking powder | 1/2 cup plain yogurt | 250g softened cream cheese | |
| 1 tsp baking soda | 3/4 cup milk mixed with 3 tsp vinegar | 1/4 cup softened butter | |
| 1/2 tsp salt | 1/4 cup water | 1 tsp vanilla | |

## Red Velvet Cupcakes

Mix together:
    2 cups flour
    1 and 1/2 cups sugar
    1 tsp baking powder
    1 tsp baking soda
    1/2 tsp salt
    3 tbsp cocoa powder

Then add in wet ingredients:
    3/4 cup canola or vegetable oil
    1/2 cup plain unsweetened yogurt (equal to 2 eggs)
    3/4 cup milk mixed with 3 tsp vinegar
    1/4 cup water
    2 tsp vanilla

Mix really well and then add in red food colouring (the amount you use is totally up to what you are comfortable with and different brands vary with the amount you use and the resulting colour. I use 1 and 1/2 tsp of liquid Club House brand) and mix well. (Note: Gel colours will result in a deeper red and require less amounts.)

Bake at 350 degrees F for approximately 20 minutes in paper-lined cupcake tins. Makes 15.

## Cream Cheese Frosting

1 pkg cream cheese (250g)
1/4 cup softened butter
1 tsp vanilla
pinch salt
3 cups icing sugar (little more if needed)

Cream together the cream cheese and the butter. Then add the vanilla, pinch of salt and the icing sugar. Beat until fluffy. Frost the cupcakes when cool.

# 8. Vanilla Cupcakes

This is an easy vanilla cupcake recipe, perfect for birthdays. These are topped with Salted Caramel Frosting.

Ingredients:

| | | | |
|---|---|---|---|
| 2 and 2/3 cups flour | 3/4 tsp salt | 1/2 cup butter | 3 cups icing sugar |
| 1/3 cup cornstarch | 3/4 cup oil | 3/4 cup brown sugar | sea salt |
| 1 and 1/2 cups white sugar | 6 tsp vanilla | 1/2 cup heavy cream (35%) | |
| 1 and 1/2 tsp baking powder | 1 and 1/4 cups milk mixed with 1 tbsp vinegar | 1/4 tsp salt | |
| 3/4 tsp baking soda | 1/2 cup plain yogurt | 1/2 tsp vanilla | |

## Vanilla Cupcakes

Sift together dry ingredients, and make a well:
  2 and 2/3 cups flour
  1/3 cup cornstarch
  1 and 1/2 cups white sugar
  1 and 1/2 tsp baking powder
  3/4 tsp baking soda
  3/4 tsp salt

Pour the wet ingredients into the well and mix until smooth:
  3/4 cup canola or vegetable oil
  6 tsp vanilla
  1 and 1/4 cups milk mixed with 1 tbsp vinegar
  1/2 cup plain unsweetened yogurt (equal to 2 eggs)

Bake at 350 degrees F for approximately 20 minutes in a cupcake tin lined with papers. Makes 18.

## Salted Caramel Frosting

Melt butter in a small saucepan and then add in the brown sugar, cream and salt:
  1/2 cup butter
  3/4 cup packed brown sugar
  1/2 cup heavy cream (35%)
  1/4 tsp salt

Make sure the sugar and the salt are dissolved and bring to a boil on medium-low heat for 2-3 minutes. Remove from heat and add in:
  1/2 tsp vanilla

Allow to cool to room temperature (reserve a small amount of caramel to drizzle), then gradually beat in the icing sugar until the consistency you want
  3 cups icing sugar

Frost the cooled cupcakes and top with a sprinkle of sea salt. (If you want lots of frosting, make an extra half batch of frosting.)

# 9. Vanilla White Chocolate Cupcakes

This is another variation of a vanilla cupcake recipe. This recipe has white chocolate in it! Chocolate helps eggless baking with texture and taste and since these are vanilla cupcakes, white chocolate is the obvious choice. I have made these for my daughter to take to school to share with her class on her birthday. These would be great for Valentine's Day as well! They are topped with a strawberry frosting which pairs well with the white chocolate in the cupcakes. This recipe does not require an egg replacer.

Ingredients:

| 1 and 3/4 cups flour | 2/3 cup sugar | 1/3 cup softened butter | 4 cups icing sugar |
|---|---|---|---|
| 1/4 cup cornstarch | 1/2 cup oil | 1/3 cup shortening | |
| 1 tsp baking powder | 3 tsp vanilla | pinch salt | |
| 1/2 tsp baking soda | 1/2 cup white chocolate chips melted | 2 tsp vanilla | |
| 1/2 tsp salt | 1 cup milk mixed with 1 tbsp vinegar | 1/4 cup strawberry puree | |

## Vanilla White Chocolate Cupcakes

In a large mixing bowl, combine:
  2/3 cup sugar
  1/2 cup canola or vegetable oil
  3 tsp vanilla

Then mix in:
  1/2 cup white chocolate chips melted

In a separate bowl, mix together the dry ingredients and set aside:
  1 and 3/4 cups flour
  1/4 cup cornstarch
  1 tsp baking powder
  1/2 tsp baking soda
  1/2 tsp salt

Slowly alternate the dry ingredients with the prepared milk mixture into the batter:
  1 cup milk mixed with 1 tbsp vinegar

Scoop into cupcake tins lined with papers. Bake at 350 degrees F for 18 to 22 minutes. Makes 12-14 large cupcakes.

## Strawberry Frosting

1/3 cup softened butter
1/3 cup shortening
pinch of salt
2 tsp vanilla
1/4 cup strawberry puree (I puree frozen strawberries in my
food processor)
4 cups icing sugar (more if needed)

Beat butter and shortening until fluffy. Then add 2 cups of the
icing sugar, the vanilla, salt, and the puree. Mix well. Add
remaining 2 cups icing sugar until it is the consistency you like.
You can add more icing sugar if needed.

# 10. Strawberry Cupcakes

Strawberry Cupcakes with Strawberry Frosting are perfect for Valentine's or a birthday party! These are moist, light and delicious!

Ingredients:

| | | | |
|---|---|---|---|
| 1/4 cup softened butter | 1 tsp vanilla | 1/2 cup milk with 1 tsp vinegar | 1/4 cup strawberry puree |
| 1 and 3/4 cups sugar | 3 cups flour | 1/3 cup softened butter | 4 cups icing sugar |
| 1/2 cup oil | 2 tsp baking powder | 1/3 cup shortening | |
| 1/2 cup plain yogurt | 1 tsp baking soda | pinch salt | |
| 1 and 1/4 cups pureed strawberries | 1/2 tsp salt | 2 tsp vanilla | |

## Strawberry Cupcakes

Cream together butter and sugar and then add the oil and mix well:
  1/4 cup softened butter
  1 and 3/4 cups sugar
  1/2 cup canola or vegetable oil

Then add in and mix well:
  1/2 cup plain unsweetened yogurt (equal to 2 eggs)
  1 and 1/4 cups pureed strawberries
  1 tsp vanilla

In a separate bowl, sift dry ingredients:
  3 cups flour
  2 tsp baking powder
  1 tsp baking soda
  1/2 tsp salt

Alternate adding dry ingredients with the milk mixture into the batter:
  1/2 cup milk mixed with 1 tsp vinegar

Mix well. Bake at 350 degrees F for approximately 20 minutes in a paper-lined cupcake tin. This is a large batch, makes 24.

## Strawberry Frosting

  1/3 cup softened butter
  1/3 cup shortening
  pinch of salt
  2 tsp vanilla
  1/4 cup strawberry puree
  4 cups icing sugar (more if needed)
Beat butter and shortening until fluffy. Then add 2 cups of the icing sugar, the vanilla, salt and the puree. Mix well. Add remaining 2 cups icing sugar until it is the consistency you like. You can add more icing sugar if needed. Note: If you want a lot of frosting, make an extra half a batch of the frosting recipe.

# 11. Quick and Easy Cupcakes

I developed this recipe to have a quick and easy eggless recipe to be able to make with my younger daughter that does not require a lot of measuring. I bought a cake mix that required the addition of eggs. Not the kind that has powdered eggs in the mix. There were not any warnings for eggs or peanuts on the box. (Make sure you always check!) The directions said to add 1/2 cup oil, and 1 cup of water or milk, and 3 eggs. I used: 1/2 cup canola oil, 1 cup water (I chose water as the yogurt is dairy), and 3/4 cup plain unsweetened yogurt. The theory is to use 1/4 cup yogurt for every egg. The mix made 14 good sized cupcakes.

These cupcakes turned out pretty good, especially since they are from a mix. It is important to use paper liners in the muffin tin. They were very light and they did not fall apart. They are a wee bit flimsy but that is partly due to the cake mix itself. I think using a chocolate based cake mix would turn out even better and sturdier due to the acidic nature of the chocolate.

Ingredients:

1 eggless boxed cake mix

water and oil (amounts asked for on the box)

1/4 cup plain yogurt for every egg required on the box

## Quick and Easy Eggless Cupcakes

1 boxed cake mix (eggless)
Add the amount of water and oil the box calls for
For every egg it asks for, add 1/4 cup plain unsweetened yogurt

Mix the ingredients together well with a mixer. Scoop into paper-lined cupcake tins. Follow the directions for baking on the package. I baked mine about 20-22 minutes at 350 degrees F. Top with your frosting of choice.

# 12. Maple Oat Muffins

You can't have too many muffin recipes. Especially if you run out of ingredients for muffins you usually make. I didn't have any ripened bananas on hand and I had just made lemon blueberry muffins, so I wanted to do something different and made oat muffins with a maple twist. I used pure maple syrup in these muffins not the artificial maple flavour, as that is just wrong!

## Ingredients:

| | |
|---|---|
| 1 and 3/4 cups flour | 1/2 tsp cinnamon |
| 1 cup oats | 1 cup milk with 1 tsp vinegar |
| 1/2 cup brown sugar | 1/3 cup oil |
| 2 tsp baking powder | 1/4 cup pure maple syrup |
| 1/4 tsp baking soda | 1/4 cup plain yogurt |
| 1/4 tsp salt | |

## Maple Oat Muffins

Sift together dry Ingredients:
  1 and 3/4 cups flour
  1 cup oats
  1/2 cup brown sugar
  2 tsp baking powder
  1/4 tsp baking soda
  1/4 tsp salt
  1/2 tsp cinnamon

In a separate bowl, combine wet ingredients:
  1 cup milk with 1 tsp vinegar
  1/3 cup canola or vegetable oil
  1/4 cup pure maple syrup
  1/4 cup plain unsweetened yogurt (or prepared egg replacer equal to 1 egg)

Mix the wet ingredients into the dry ingredients and stir until just combined. Bake in a paper-lined muffin tin for 18-20 minutes at 400 degrees F. Makes 12.

# 13. Coconut Lime Muffins

A sale on limes at the grocery store and a few bags of coconut in the fridge is the inspiration for these muffins, along with an upcoming camping trip! Yum!

Ingredients:

| | | |
|---|---|---|
| 2 cups flour | zest of one lime | 1 cup unsweetened coconut |
| 3/4 cup sugar | 1/2 cup oil | |
| 2 tsp baking powder | 1/2 cup milk | |
| 1/2 tsp baking soda | 1/2 cup plain Greek yogurt | |
| 1/2 tsp salt | 2 tbsp lime juice | |

## Coconut Lime Muffins

Sift together dry ingredients:
  2 cups flour
  3/4 cup sugar
  2 tsp baking powder
  1/2 tsp baking soda
  1/2 tsp salt
  zest of a large lime

In a separate bowl, combine the wet ingredients:
  1/2 cup canola oil
  1/2 cup milk
  1/2 cup plain unsweetened Greek yogurt (equal to 2 eggs)
  2 tbsp lime juice

Mix the wet and dry ingredients together until just incorporated. Spoon into a paper-lined muffin tin and top each muffin with a sprinkle of unsweetened coconut.

Bake at 375 degrees F for approximately 20 mins*. Makes 12.

*Note: Keep an eye on the muffins while baking and if the coconut is getting too brown, cover with parchment paper.

# 14. Pumpkin Whole Wheat Muffins

These whole wheat muffins are a great breakfast item or snack choice. They are made with whole wheat flour, honey and nutrient-packed pumpkin. They only contain half a cup of brown sugar and are really moist.

Ingredients:

| | | |
|---|---|---|
| 2 cups whole wheat flour | 1 tsp cinnamon | 1/2 cup honey |
| 1/2 cup brown sugar | 1/4 tsp nutmeg | 1 cup pumpkin puree |
| 1 tsp baking powder | 1/4 tsp allspice | 1/4 cup oil |
| 1/2 tsp baking soda | 1/2 cup plain yogurt | |
| 1/2 tsp salt | 1/2 cup milk | |

## Pumpkin Whole Wheat Muffins

Sift together dry ingredients in a large bowl:
  2 cups whole wheat flour
  1/2 cup brown sugar
  1 tsp baking powder
  1/2 tsp baking soda
  1/2 tsp salt
  1 tsp cinnamon
  1/4 tsp nutmeg
  1/4 tsp allspice

In a separate bowl, combine wet ingredients and then add into dry ingredients:
  1/2 cup unsweetened plain yogurt (or prepared egg replacer equal to 2 eggs)
  1/2 cup milk
  1/2 cup honey
  1 cup pumpkin puree
  1/4 cup canola or vegetable oil
Mix until just combined and spoon into paper-lined muffin tins.
Makes 14 large muffins.
Bake at 400 degrees F for 18-20 minutes.

# 15. Raspberry Lemon Muffins

I make these muffins with half whole wheat flour as they are a good option for my daughter's school lunch and she refuses to eat sandwiches. She will however eat muffins, unless they are banana muffins. She will eat banana muffins if they have chocolate chips in them.......you get my point?

Ingredients:

| 1 cup whole wheat flour | 1 tsp baking soda | 1/3 cup milk |
|---|---|---|
| 1 cup white flour | 1/2 tsp salt | 2 tbsp lemon juice |
| 2 tbsp flax seed meal | zest 1 lemon | 1 tsp vanilla |
| 3/4 cup white sugar | 1/2 cup plain yogurt | 1 and 1/2 cups raspberries |
| 2 tsp baking powder | 1/4 cup oil | |

# Raspberry Lemon Muffins

Combine dry ingredients:
   1 cup whole wheat flour
   1 cup white flour
   2 tbsp flax seed meal
   3/4 cup white sugar
   2 tsp baking powder
   1 tsp baking soda
   1/2 tsp salt
   zest of 1 lemon

Combine wet ingredients in a separate bowl, and then mix into the dry ingredients until just combined:
   1/2 cup plain sweetened yogurt (equal to 2 eggs)
   1/4 cup canola or vegetable oil
   1/3 cup milk
   2 tbsp lemon juice
   1 tsp vanilla

Then fold in:
   1 and 1/2 cups frozen or fresh raspberries

Bake at 400 degrees F for 18-20 minutes in a paper-lined muffin tin. Makes 12.

# 16. Lemon Blueberry Muffins

These muffins are yummy, light and bright. The combination of blueberries and lemon is classic. This muffin recipe is one of my personal favourites!

Ingredients:

| 2 cups flour | zest of 1 lemon | 1 cup blueberries dusted with flour |
| --- | --- | --- |
| 3/4 cup sugar | 1 cup plain yogurt | |
| 2 tsp baking powder | 1/2 cup oil | |
| 1 tsp baking soda | 1/4 cup lemon juice | |
| 1/2 tsp salt | 1 tsp vanilla | |

## Lemon Blueberry Muffins

Combine dry ingredients:
   2 cups flour
   3/4 cup sugar
   2 tsp baking powder
   1 tsp baking soda
   1/2 tsp salt
   zest of 1 large lemon

In a separate bowl, combine wet ingredients:
   1 cup plain unsweetened yogurt (equal to 4 eggs)
   1/2 cup canola or vegetable oil
   1/4 cup lemon juice
   1 tsp vanilla

Add wet ingredients to the dry and mix until just combined. Then fold in:
   1 cup frozen or fresh blueberries dusted with flour

Bake at 400 degrees F in a paper-lined muffin tin for approximately 18-20 minutes. Makes 12.

# 17. Blueberry White Chocolate Muffins

Some of the best recipes come out of leftover bits of food you have on hand. The rest of a bag of frozen blueberries, the remainder of a bag of white chocolate chips, a lemon you haven't used........ These really are a cross between a muffin and a cupcake. Definitely more of a dessert than a breakfast muffin but I am sure your kids will try and talk you into having them for breakfast!

Ingredients:

| | |
|---|---|
| 1/2 cup softened butter | 1 and 1/2 tsp baking powder |
| 3/4 cup sugar | 1/2 tsp salt |
| 3/4 cup plain yogurt | 1/2 cup milk |
| zest and juice of 1 lemon | 1/2 cup white chocolate chips |
| 2 cups flour | 1 cup blueberries dusted with flour |

## Blueberry White Chocolate Muffins

Cream together:
    1/2 cup butter softened
    3/4 cup sugar

Then add and mix well:
    3/4 cup plain unsweetened yogurt (equal to 3 eggs)
    zest and juice of one lemon

In a separate bowl, combine dry ingredients:
    2 cups flour
    1 and 1/2 tsp baking powder
    1/2 tsp salt

Alternate adding the dry ingredients with the milk into the batter until incorporated:
    1/2 cup milk

Then fold in:
    1/2 cup white chocolate chips
    1 cup blueberries dusted with flour

Bake at 350 degrees F for approximately 25 minutes in a paper-lined muffin tin. Makes 12.

# 18. Banana Chocolate Chip Muffins

This is my go-to Banana Muffin recipe that I have used for years. I always add a bit of vinegar in with the milk to help them rise a little higher as bananas tend to weigh muffins down. The kids will eat pretty much anything if there's chocolate chips involved so these muffins are always a hit!

Ingredients:

| | |
|---|---|
| 1 and 3/4 cups flour | 3/4 cup chocolate chips |
| 1/4 cup white sugar | 1/4 cup plain yogurt |
| 1/4 cup brown sugar | 1/4 cup oil |
| 1 tbsp baking powder | 1/3 cup milk with 1 tsp vinegar |
| 1/2 tsp salt | 3 mashed bananas |

## Banana Chocolate Chip Muffins

Mix together dry ingredients:
    1 and 3/4 cups flour
    1/4 cup white sugar
    1/4 cup brown sugar
    1 tbsp baking powder
    1/2 tsp salt
    3/4 cup chocolate chips

In a separate bowl mix together the wet ingredients:
    1/4 cup plain unsweetened yogurt (or egg replacer equal to 1 egg)
    1/4 cup canola or vegetable oil
    1/3 cup milk mixed with 1 tsp vinegar
    3 mashed bananas

Combine the wet and dry ingredients until just incorporated. Scoop batter into a paper-lined muffin tin. Fill the cups two-thirds full. Makes 12.

Bake at 400 degrees F for approximately 20 minutes.

# 19. Whole Wheat Banana Chip Muffins

These are rustic looking but very good whole wheat muffins. I use ground flax seed meal in these which helps with egg replacement in addition to adding extra nutrients. This is a whole wheat variation of my Banana Chip Muffin recipe. These are perfect for breakfast!

Ingredients:

| | |
|---|---|
| 2 cups whole wheat flour (less 2 tbsp) | 3/4 cup chocolate chips |
| 2 tbsp flax seed meal | 1/4 cup plain yogurt |
| 1/2 cup brown sugar | 1/4 cup oil |
| 1 tbsp baking powder | 1/3 cup milk mixed with 1 tsp vinegar |
| 1/2 tsp salt | 3 mashed bananas |

## Whole Wheat Banana Chip Muffins

Combine dry ingredients:
   2 cups whole wheat flour (less 2 tbsp)
   2 tbsp ground flax seed meal
   1/2 cup brown sugar
   1 tbsp baking powder
   1/2 tsp salt
   3/4 cup chocolate chips

In a separate bowl, mix together wet ingredients:
   1/4 cup plain yogurt (or egg replacer equal to 1 egg)
   1/4 cup canola oil
   1/3 cup milk mixed with 1 tsp vinegar
   3 mashed bananas

Add the wet ingredients to the dry and mix until just combined. Scoop into a paper-lined muffin tin. Bake at 400 degrees F for approximately 20 minutes. Makes 12.

# 20. Maple Banana Muffins

Since Friday is grocery day in my house, I always find myself on Wednesday or Thursday either having to go to the grocery store or use what I have in the cupboard to bake something for the kid's lunches for school. This recipe came about on such a day and wanting to try something different, I experimented with making Maple Banana Muffins. I made them healthier by using half whole wheat flour and flax seed, which combined with the yogurt, adds protein that is missing from not using eggs.

Ingredients:

| 1 cup whole wheat flour | 1/4 tsp baking soda | 1 cup mashed bananas |
| --- | --- | --- |
| 1 cup white flour | 1/4 tsp salt | 1 tsp vanilla |
| 2 tbsp flax seed meal | 1/2 cup plain yogurt | |
| 1/4 cup brown sugar | 1/4 cup oil | |
| 2 tsp baking powder | 1/2 cup maple syrup | |

# Maple Banana Muffins

Combine dry ingredients:
  1 cup whole wheat flour
  1 cup white flour
  2 tbsp ground flax seed meal
  1/4 cup brown sugar
  2 tsp baking powder
  1/4 tsp baking soda
  1/4 tsp salt

In a separate bowl, combine the wet ingredients:
  1/2 cup plain unsweetened yogurt (or egg replacer equal to 2 eggs)
  1/4 cup canola oil
  1/2 cup maple syrup
  1 cup mashed bananas (2 large or 3 medium)
  1 tsp vanilla

Mix together the wet and dry ingredients until just incorporated. Bake at 400 degrees F for approximately 20 minutes in a paper-lined muffin tin. Makes 12.

These smell amazing as they are baking!

# 21. Banana Oat Muffins

I like to make these up and freeze them for lunches or for on the go mid-morning snacks. Oats and flax seed make these nutritious in addition to being yummy!

Ingredients:

| 1 and 1/2 cups flour | 1 tsp baking soda | 1 tsp vanilla |
|---|---|---|
| 1 cup oats | 1/2 tsp salt | 3 mashed bananas |
| 2 tbsp flaxseed meal | 1/2 cup plain yogurt | |
| 1/2 cup sugar | 1/4 cup oil | |
| 2 tsp baking powder | 1/3 cup milk with 1 tsp vinegar | |

## Banana Oat Muffins

Mix together dry ingredients:
- 1 and 1/2 cups flour
- 1 cup oats
- 2 tbsp ground flax seed meal
- 1/2 cup sugar
- 2 tsp baking powder
- 1 tsp baking soda
- 1/2 tsp salt

In a separate bowl, combine wet ingredients:
- 1/2 cup plain unsweetened yogurt (or egg replacer equal to 2 eggs)
- 1/4 cup canola oil
- 1/3 cup milk mixed with 1 tsp vinegar
- 1 tsp vanilla
- 3 medium mashed bananas

Add the wet ingredients to the dry ingredients and mix until just combined. Spoon into paper-lined muffin tins. Makes 14 large muffins. Bake at 400 degrees F for approximately 18-20 minutes.

# 22. Pumpkin Chocolate Chip Muffins

To make these muffins I often use whole pumpkins. I just halve a sugar pumpkin, scoop out the seeds and place it upside down in a baking dish and cover it with foil. I bake it for 1 and half hours at 400 degrees F. It's by far easier than slicing and peeling a hard pumpkin. It also turns out drier than traditionally steamed pumpkin that is cooked on the stove top. Once the pumpkin cools a bit, I scoop it out and puree it in the food processor. If you don't want to use fresh pumpkin, canned pumpkin will also be good and the pumpkin flavour will be a bit more concentrated.

Ingredients:

| | | |
|---|---|---|
| 2 cups flour | 1/2 tsp salt | 1/2 cup plain yogurt |
| 1/2 cup brown sugar | 1 tsp cinnamon | 1/3 cup oil |
| 1/4 cup white sugar | 1/4 tsp nutmeg | 1/3 cup milk |
| 1 tsp baking powder | 1/4 tsp allspice | 1 and 1/2 cups pumpkin puree |
| 1/2 tsp baking soda | 3/4 cup chocolate chips | |

## Pumpkin Chocolate Chip Muffins

Combine dry Ingredients:
  2 cups flour
  1/2 cup packed brown sugar
  1/4 cup white sugar
  1 tsp baking powder
  1/2 tsp baking soda
  1/2 tsp salt
  1 tsp cinnamon
  1/4 tsp nutmeg
  1/4 tsp allspice
  3/4 cup chocolate chips

In a separate bowl, combine the wet ingredients:
  1/2 cup plain unsweetened yogurt (or egg replacer equal to 2 eggs)
  1/3 cup canola or vegetable oil
  1/3 cup milk
  1 and 1/2 cups pumpkin puree

Combine the wet and dry ingredients. Stir only to moisten. Bake at 400 degrees F for 20 minutes in a paper-lined muffin tin. Makes 12 large muffins.

# 23. Blueberry Oat Muffins

If you are like me, I am always looking for muffin recipes for breakfasts and school lunches. My kids love blueberries so they will eat these up in no time. These are not very sweet muffins so they are perfect for breakfasts as they are low in added sugars.

Ingredients:

| 1 and 1/2 cups flour | 1/2 tsp salt | 1 tsp vanilla |
| --- | --- | --- |
| 1 cup oats | 1/4 tsp cinnamon | 1 cup blueberries |
| 2 tbsp flax seed meal | 1/2 cup plain yogurt | |
| 1/3 cup brown sugar | 1/4 cup oil | |
| 1 tbsp baking powder | 1 cup milk | |

# Blueberry Oat Muffins

Combine dry ingredients:
   1 and 1/2 cups flour
   1 cup oats
   2 tbsp ground flax seed meal
   1/3 cup packed brown sugar
   1 tbsp baking powder
   1/2 tsp salt
   1/4 tsp cinnamon

In a separate bowl, combine wet ingredients:
   1/2 cup plain yogurt (or egg replacer equal to 2 eggs)
   1/4 cup canola or vegetable oil
   1 cup milk
   1 tsp vanilla

Stir together wet and dry ingredients only until just mixed, then fold in:
   1 cup blueberries dusted with flour

Spoon into a paper-lined muffin tin. Bake at 400 degrees F for approximately 20 minutes. Makes 12.

# 24. Mango Blueberry Oat Muffins

The combination of mango and blueberries in these muffins is delicious. The inspiration for these muffins was a slightly under ripe mango that was a little tart. If you like coconut, you could add 1/4 cup in this recipe.

Ingredients:

| | | |
|---|---|---|
| 1 and 1/2 cups flour | 1/4 tsp salt | 1 tsp vanilla |
| 1/2 cup oats | 1/4 cup plain yogurt | 1 mango diced |
| 1/2 cup sugar | 1/2 cup sour cream | 1/2 cup blueberries |
| 2 tbsp flax seed meal | 1/2 cup milk | |
| 1 and 1/2 tsp baking powder | 1/2 cup oil | |

# Mango Blueberry Oat Muffins

Combine dry ingredients:
- 1 and 1/2 cups flour
- 1/2 cup oats
- 1/2 cup sugar
- 2 tbsp ground flax seed meal
- 1 and 1/2 tsp baking powder
- 1/4 tsp salt

In a separate bowl, combine wet ingredients:
- 1/4 cup plain unsweetened yogurt (or egg replacer equal to 1 egg)
- 1/2 cup sour cream
- 1/2 cup milk
- 1/2 cup canola or vegetable oil
- 1 tsp vanilla

Mix together wet and dry ingredients until just combined. Then gently mix in 1 diced mango and a 1/2 cup of blueberries. Spoon into a muffin tin lined with paper cups and top with a sprinkling of large flake oats.

Bake at 375 degrees F for approximately 25 minutes in a paper-lined muffin tin. Makes 12.

# Inspiration

*My 14 year old son was diagnosed with an egg and peanut allergy when he was 11 months old. He cannot eat eggs in any form. I have been baking and cooking without eggs since then. I adapt recipes and have been able to recreate baked goods which receive great reviews from family and friends alike. Hopefully this book will be helpful for many families out there who have a child or a family member with an egg allergy and need some help getting started baking, cooking and living eggless.*

# About the Author

*I am a stay at home mother of three, one of whom is allergic to eggs and peanuts. I have been cooking and baking without eggs for over 13 years with many successes! I hope to help families who have just discovered their child is allergic to eggs by creating recipes that really work and that do not compromise on taste!*

Enjoy!

*Jacquelynn Spinney*
myegglessworld.com

https://www.facebook.com/MyEgglessWorld

Printed in Great Britain
by Amazon